The Urbana Free Library

To renew: call **217-367-4057**
or go to **urbanafreelibrary.org**
and select **My Account**

THE DECLARATION OF INDEPENDENCE

by Marcia Abramson

BEARPORT
PUBLISHING

Minneapolis, Minnesota

Credits:
© Cover: clockwise from bottom left, Mather Brown/Public Domain; Russ/Creative Commons; Yellowj/Shutterstock; Joseph Sohm/Shutterstock.com; Raul Baena/Shutterstock; Title Page top, Jean Leon Gerome Ferris/Library of Congress/Public Domain; Title Page bottom, 22, Harvey Barrison/Creative Commons; TOC, 10 right, Howard Chandler Christy/Public Domain; 4, Howard Pyle/Public Domain; 5 top, Johannes Adam Simon Oertel/Public Domain; 5 bottom, S Pakhrin/Creative Commons; 5 top right, JLauer/Shutterstock.com; 5 bottom right, Jim Lambert/Shutterstock.com; 6 top, John White/Public Domain; 6 bottom, National Park Service/Public Domain; p 7, Royal Collection of the United Kingdom/Public Domain; 8, Kevin M. McCarthy/Shutterstock.com; 9 top, Karl Anton Hickel/Public Domain; 9 top right, 9 bottom left, 23 bottom left, Ken Schulze/Shutterstock.com; 9 bottom right, Natalia Chuen/Shutterstock.com; 10 left, Talvi/Shutterstock; 10 middle, Jean Leon Gerome Ferris/Public Domain; 11 top, Nathaniel Currier/Public Domain; 11 bottom left, Verena Joy/Shutterstock.com; 11 right, turtix/Shutterstock; 12, NYPL/Public Domain; 13 top, John Trumbull/Public Domain; 13 middle left, Yellowj/Shutterstock; 13 bottom, Domenick D'Andrea/Public Domain; 13 right, Jim.henderson/Creative Commons; 14 left, Edward Savages/Public Domain; 14 right, 21 bottom right, Allan Ramsay/Public Domain; 15 top, Gilbert Stuart/Public Domain; 15 bottom, Rtguest/Dreamstime.com; 15 left, Charles Willson Peale/Public Domain; 15 top left, The Library of Congress/Public Domain; 15 right, Workshop of William Beechey/Public Domain; 16, U.S. National Archives and Records Administration/Public Domain; 16 top, John Singleton Copley/Public Domain; 17 left, Daderot/Creative Commons; 17 right Currier & Ives/Public Domain; 18, John Trumbull/Public Domain; 19 bottom, Jean Leon Gerome Ferris/Public Domain; 19 right, bonchan/Shutterstock; 19 top left, Gift of Mrs. Robert Homans/Public Domain; 19 top right, Gilbert Stuart/Public Domain; 20, The White House Historical Association (White House Collection)/Public Domain; 21 bottom left, John Singleton Copley/Public Domain; 21 bottom right, Izanbar/Dreamstime.com; 21 top left, Joseph Siffrein/Public Domain; 21 top right, 25 middle right, National Park Service/Public Domain; 23 bottom middle, Digital Storm/Shutterstock; 23 bottom, Chris Light/Creative Commons; 23 top, The U.S. National Archives/Flickr Commons; 23 middle, Public Domain; 24, U.S. National Archives/Public Domain; 24 left, stockfour/Shutterstock; 24 right, Billion Photos/Shutterstock; 25 bottom, Creative Commons; 25 top Lou Oates/Shutterstock; 26 top, Public Domain; 26 bottom, Richard Cavalleri/Shutterstock; 27 left, Zhukovsky/Dreamstime.com; 27 top, Public Domain; ESB Professional/Shutterstock; 28 left, Shaiith/Shutterstock; 29 bottom left, Eric Isselee/Shutterstock; 28-29, Austen Photography

Developed and produced for Bearport Publishing by BlueAppleWorks Inc.
Managing Editor for BlueAppleWorks: Melissa McClellan
Art Director: T.J. Choleva
Photo Research: Jane Reid
Editor: Jane Yates

Library of Congress Cataloging-in-Publication Data

Names: Abramson, Marcia, 1949– author.
Title: The Declaration of Independence / by Marcia Abramson.
Description: Minneapolis, Minnesota : Bearport Publishing Company, [2021] |
    Series: Xtreme facts: history | Includes bibliographical references and
    index.
Identifiers: LCCN 2020012979 (print) | LCCN 2020012980 (ebook) | ISBN
    9781647471200 (library binding) | ISBN 9781647471279 (paperback) | ISBN
    9781647471347 (ebook)
Subjects: LCSH: United States. Declaration of Independence—Juvenile
    literature. | United States—Politics and
    government—1775-1783—Miscellanea—Juvenile literature.
Classification: LCC E221 .A27 2021 (print) | LCC E221 (ebook) | DDC
    973.3/13—dc23
LC record available at https://lccn.loc.gov/2020012979
LC ebook record available at https://lccn.loc.gov/2020012980

Contents

A Particular Piece of Paper

The 13 American **colonies** declared independence from England on July 4, 1776. On that date, one of the most famous documents in U.S. history was born—the Declaration of Independence. The next day, riders on horseback began taking copies to all the colonies. When General George Washington received his copy, he was thrilled. One of his men read the Declaration of Independence to Washington's soldiers.

News about the declaration didn't reach England until **August 10**!

I HAVE SOME GOOD NEWS!

The word **independence** never appears in the document!

General Washington was in New York when he got his copy of the declaration.

4

Crowds who heard the news were so happy they knocked down a statue of King George III. Then, they **cut off the statue's head!**

SEE YA LATER, KING GEORGE!

The crowd used ropes to pull the statue down.

The country celebrates the declaration and what it stood for every July 4.

The colonists melted down King George's statue to make bullets—**42,088 bullets**, to be exact!

Before There Were States

But wait—what exactly were these 13 colonies? In the 1600s, England and other countries sent people to explore, live, and work in the Americas. They formed groups, or colonies, to grow **crops** and trade goods that would make money for the home countries. During the 1700s, the colonies from England grew, and a group of them became the 13 original American colonies.

Many of the colonies were built on **Native American** lands. Some Native Americans fought back against the **colonists**.

The first English settlements had only a few hundred people. But, by 1775, 2.4 million people lived in the 13 colonies.

The first English settlement vanished mysteriously! Settlers came to Roanoke Island, near North Carolina, in 1587. Three years later, nothing was left of the colony.

The colonies would later become the states of Connecticut, Delaware, Georgia, New Hampshire, New Jersey, New York, North Carolina, Maryland, Massachusetts, Pennsylvania, Rhode Island, South Carolina, and Virginia.

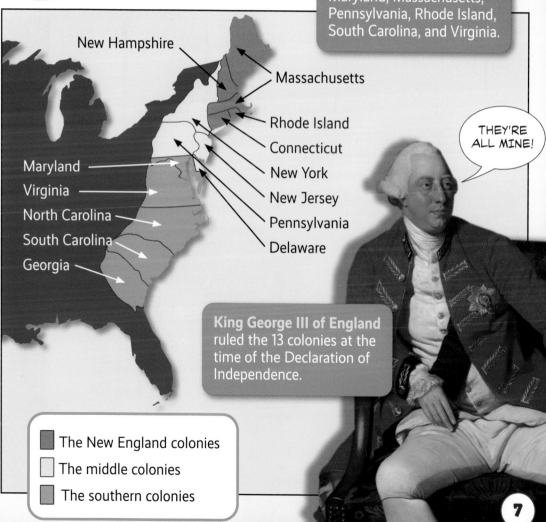

New Hampshire

Massachusetts

Rhode Island

Connecticut

New York

New Jersey

Pennsylvania

Delaware

Maryland

Virginia

North Carolina

South Carolina

Georgia

THEY'RE ALL MINE!

King George III of England ruled the 13 colonies at the time of the Declaration of Independence.

The New England colonies

The middle colonies

The southern colonies

No Taxation Without Representation!

England was getting a lot of money from its colonies. But, by the 1760s, many colonists were wondering if they were getting enough back.

After a long and expensive war with France, England decided it needed more money. It **imposed** new **taxes** on the colonies. The colonists grew angry. They decided if they had to *pay* the money, the colonists should get to take part in the government that *received* the money. Some colonists began a **boycott** of English goods so they wouldn't have to pay the taxes.

A TOAST TO OUR NEW TAXES!

YOU NASTY TAX COLLECTORS!

In 1765, nine men in Boston formed a secret group called the Sons of Liberty to **protest**. They didn't like the taxes or the tax collectors.

England made many laws to control the colonies. There was even **a law that kept the colonists from making hats!**

Along with the king, a group called Parliament ruled Britain and its colonies.

NOW WE HAVE TO PAY TAXES ON PLAYING CARDS?!

CAN YOU BELIEVE IT?

Colonists used the phrase "No taxation without representation" while they protested. The saying was probably first used in Ireland, which was treated like a British colony.

IRELAND

ENGLAND

Even playing cards were taxed under one of the new laws.

Fighting Taxes and Throwing Tea

Most colonists paid the taxes forced on them by the British until England passed the Tea Act in 1773. People in the colonies loved to drink tea—and they drank a lot of it.

A group of colonists in Boston, Massachusetts, were very angry about the new tax and decided to take action. They snuck onto British ships and dumped hundreds of crates of tea into Boston Harbor. This famous event became known as the Boston Tea Party.

Benjamin Franklin offered to pay for the tea that was destroyed with his own money if the tax law was **revoked**. It wasn't, so Franklin kept his money.

I'LL PAY.

(MAYBE)

More than 90,000 pounds (44,820 kg) of tea was thrown into Boston Harbor. That's about the weight of 14 elephants!

George Washington didn't support what happened in Boston.

Colonists cheered as tea was thrown into the harbor.

The War Begins!

The British punished the colonies for their tax protests by creating harsh new rules, especially for Massachusetts. In response, the colonists sent representatives to a large meeting in Philadelphia, Pennsylvania. This meeting became the First Continental Congress. The congress wrote to King George III to ask him to stop the harsh treatment. Nothing changed.

In 1775, colonists fought against British soldiers who stormed the Massachusetts towns of Lexington and Concord to search for hidden weapons. Soon after, the Second Continental Congress decided to fight against the British in the Revolutionary War (1775-1783).

The colonists were huge underdogs! England had a larger population, more money, and a stronger army.

The French, Spanish, and Dutch also entered the war. They fought with the American colonists against the British.

The first shots of the Revolutionary War were fired in Lexington on April 19, 1775.

The war lasted eight years, until a peace **treaty** was finally signed in 1783.

The fighting ended when Britain surrendered at Yorktown, Virginia.

Colonists called British soldiers Redcoats and Lobsters because they wore bright red coats.

WHAT DID YOU JUST CALL ME?

The colonists who supported the war against England were known as **patriots**.

George Vs. George

The American Revolution was a battle of Georges. The British were led by King George III. The colonies were led by General George Washington. When it came to actually joining in the war, however, the two Georges were quite different. The king stayed in England, an ocean away from the fighting and danger. General Washington was on the battlefield, fighting alongside his men in any way he could.

Washington was a **descendant** of King Edward I of England. Some people wanted to make him the **king of the United States!**

HMM.

WE'RE FAMILY!

King George III first met his wife, and future queen, on their wedding day!

George Washington became the first president of the United States. He served two terms and was hugely popular.

THEY REALLY LIKE ME!

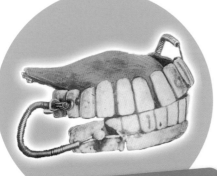

George Washington wore false teeth. They probably included cow, horse, and human teeth!

King George III wasn't happy about losing the war. He even wrote a speech that basically said "I QUIT!" But he never gave his speech and ruled for nearly 60 years.

WHERE IS GEORGE?

OVER HERE, GEORGE!

ENGLAND

USA

General Washington and King George III never met nor set foot in each other's country.

Minutemen and Founding Women

Some of the first soldiers in the revolution were known as minutemen—because they could be ready at a minute's notice. They were members of **militias**, or smaller groups of fighters, who lived in the areas where they fought. Because they were local, they knew the **terrain** much better than the British.

Paul Revere was probably the most famous minuteman. Late on April 18, 1775, he rode on horseback from Boston to Lexington to warn the colonists that the British were coming.

THE BRITISH ARE COMING!

THANKS FOR THE HEADS-UP!

In 1777, another rider helped warn colonists about British soldiers. Sybil Ludington was just 16 when she rode 40 miles (64 km) in the middle of the night!

While men were fighting, many women continued to care for their homes and children. And some women marched right along with the army. They helped with cooking, washing clothes, and nursing wounded soldiers. A few women even joined British camps and spied for the Americans!

A famous war story tells of a woman named **Molly Pitcher** who took over firing her husband's cannon when he was injured!

For 17 months, Deborah Sampson dressed as a man, used a fake name, and fought in battles alongside her fellow patriots.

A minuteman statue stands guard in Lexington. It shows Captain John Parker, who led the militia in battle.

A Reluctant Writer

The colonists wanted the whole world to know why they were fighting and what kind of nation they hoped to create. When the Second Continental Congress met in 1776, they selected five men to draft a document that explained the colonists' thinking. Those men were John Adams, Thomas Jefferson, Benjamin Franklin, Robert Livingston, and Roger Sherman. The group then chose Jefferson to write the first draft.

Thomas Jefferson thought John Adams would be a better choice to write the first draft, but Adams replied that Jefferson was ten times a better writer!

Jefferson and Adams both died on July 4, 1826. That date was also the 50th anniversary of the Declaration of Independence.

Robert Livingston

Thomas Jefferson

Roger Sherman

Benjamin Franklin

John Adams

The five-man writing committee of the Declaration of Independence presented their final draft to the congress on June 28, 1776.

Abigail Adams urged her husband, John Adams, to include women in the Declaration of Independence.

JOHN, REMEMBER THE LADIES, PLEASE!

YES, DEAR.

Even though **Jefferson** wrote the declaration, he refused to read it out loud. He spoke with a lisp and was too shy to speak in public.

Jefferson loved ice cream. He even wrote the first ice cream recipe in America.

Benjamin Franklin was also famous for his writing, but he put on his editor's hat when it came to the declaration. He made small changes to what Jefferson originally wrote.

Signers of the Times

After it was ratified, or approved, by the Second Continental Congress, the Declaration of Independence was signed on July 4, 1776. Only John Hancock, the president of the congress, and Charles Thomson, the secretary, wrote their names on the document.

Then, they ordered another copy to be written more clearly. This new **parchment** copy had another important feature: room for all of the delegates to sign their names. On August 2, the delegates began signing the new copy.

I HOPE MY GIANT **SIGNATURE** CAPTURES THE KING'S EYE.

John Hancock's signature on the Declaration of Independence was big! Since that day, signatures are often called John Hancocks.

SHOW-OFF!

All but eight of the delegates who signed the declaration were born in the colonies.

All 56 delegates of the Second Continental Congress signed the Declaration of Independence.

England considered **signing the Declaration of Independence an act of treason**, which could result in the signers' execution!

Benjamin Franklin was a scientist, an inventor, and a printer!

OLDEST HERE!

YOUNGEST HERE!

At 70, Benjamin Franklin was the oldest person to sign. **The youngest signer was Edward Rutledge**. He was only 26 years old.

Copies, Copies, Everywhere!

The original Declaration of Independence has been a frequent traveler. At first, it went wherever the Continental Congress did. In 1789, the Department of State took possession of the declaration. In 1921, the document was handed over to the Library of Congress.

But there wasn't just one copy of the Declaration of Independence. Many copies were made at different times and for different reasons.

The original declaration has been folded and rolled so many times that **most of the original ink has come off!**

YES, IT'S FOLDED NEATLY IN MY SADDLEBAG.

DO YOU HAVE THE DECLARATION?

The approved declaration
On July 4, 1776, this version was approved by the Second Continental Congress. It was signed only by John Hancock and Charles Thomson.

Dunlap broadsides
The following morning, printer John Dunlap made around 200 large paper copies of the document, called **broadsides**, to send around to the colonies.

Newspaper versions
Several newspapers printed their own versions of the declaration in the following days and weeks.

The signed version
An official copy with space for signatures at the bottom was finished on August 2. This is the copy that traveled with the Continental Congress.

Goddard broadsides
More copies were made in 1777 by Mary Katherine Goddard, a printer and the first female postmaster. They were the first official copies with all the signatures.

The stone engraving
In 1820, William J. Stone was hired to make an engraving of the fully signed document, whose ink was already beginning to fade. He made about 200 copies. These versions are used for most copies today.

There are 26 known copies of the **Dunlap broadside** today.

BALTIMORE, IN MARYLAND: Printed by MARY KATHARINE GODDARD.

When Mary Katherine Goddard printed her broadsides, she added a line with her own name, too!

During World War II, the signed declaration was sent to Fort Knox, in Kentucky, for safe-keeping. This is also where a lot of the U.S. gold is kept!

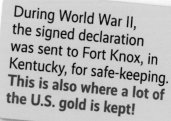

IS THE DECLARATION SAFE?

GOOD AS GOLD!

A Handprint Mystery

The Declaration of Independence is an extremely important document, and for many years it was well cared for. A photograph of the signed version was taken in 1903. The copy was 127 years old, but it appeared to be in good shape. However, in a 1940 photograph, historians saw that the document was much dirtier and looked as if it had gotten wet. Even more mysterious was a handprint that could be seen in the lower left corner!

LOOK AT THE HANDPRINT! HOW DID THAT HAPPEN?

I DON'T KNOW. IT'S *HANDY* THAT WE HAVE OTHER COPIES!

In another photo mystery, we've lost the first photo of the Declaration of Independence. It was taken in 1883, but nobody knows where the photo is today.

The signatures on the document have gotten much harder to read over the years.

There's one place where the signatures may never fade. Each of the original signatures is carved in stone at a memorial in Washington, D.C.

The Memorial to the 56 Signers of the Declaration of Independence is located in the Constitution Gardens on the National Mall in Washington, D.C.

The Declaration Today

Although the Declaration of Independence is nearly 250 years old, it's still important to the lives of people today. The declaration reminds people that everyone was created equal and that we all have certain rights that cannot be taken away. Today, after more than 25 moves, the Declaration of Independence is on display at the National Archives in Washington, D.C.

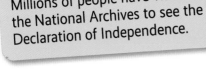

Millions of people have visited the National Archives to see the Declaration of Independence.

The National Archives

The declaration was the first text to be **digitized** and uploaded onto what would one day become the internet.

The declaration helped to inspire the French to fight for their own freedom. They wrote their "Declaration of the Rights of Man" in 1789.

The **Freedom Tower** at the One World Trade Center in New York City **is 1,776 feet (541 m) high**, in honor of the year the declaration was signed.

More than 200 years after the Declaration of Independence was signed, a man discovered a Dunlap broadside behind a painting **he bought at a flea marked for $4!** He sold the copy for $2.1 million in 1991.

JACKPOT!

Freedom Feather
CRAFT PROJECT

The Declaration of Independence would not have been written without birds! In the 1700s, people used pens made from long feathers of ducks, geese, turkeys, and other large birds. These pens were called quills.

Make your own quill pen to see how people wrote in the colonial era. It wasn't easy! Practice writing with some words from the declaration.

What You Will Need

- Large feathers (available at most craft stores)
- Scissors
- A toothpick
- Water
- A small bottle or bowl
- Food coloring
- Paper

Quills wore down quickly, but the colonists raised lots of ducks and geese. Feathers were not hard to find.

Step One

Select a large craft feather with a hollow center. With the scissors, cut the tip of the feather at a diagonal angle. Clean inside the hollow part with a toothpick. This will help the feather hold the ink for writing.

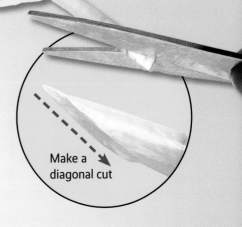

Make a diagonal cut

Step Two

Pour a small amount of water into your jar or bowl. Add a few drops of food coloring to the water.

Step Three

Dip the end of your quill pen into the dyed-water ink and begin writing! You'll have to re-dip every few letters.

We hold these truths to be self-evident: That all men are created equal

Along with the declaration, **Thomas Jefferson wrote 20,000 letters in his life!** He raised special geese at his farm so he would have enough good quills.

Glossary

boycott to refuse to buy something or deal with someone

broadsides large sheets of paper printed on one side

colonies areas that have been settled by people from another country and are ruled by that country

colonists people living in a colony

crops plants that are grown as food

descendant a person related to someone who lived earlier

digitized created in an electronic version to be stored on a computer

imposed caused something, such as taxes or rules, to affect people by using official power

militias groups of citizens who organize for military purposes but are not usually part of the official army

Native Americans the first inhabitants of the Americas

parchment a type of paper made from animal skin

protest an act or declaration of disagreement and objection

revoked taken back or canceled

signature a person's name, handwritten in a unique way

taxes money paid to a government so that it can provide services to the people

terrain the physical features of a piece of land, such as hills, forests, and rivers

treaty an official written agreement to resolve a dispute between nations

Read More

Harris, Michael C. *What Is the Declaration of Independence?* New York: Grosset & Dunlap (2016).

Keppeler, Jill. *Team Time Machine Drafts the Declaration of Independence (Team Time Machine: American Revolution).* New York: Gareth Stevens Publishing (2020).

Leavitt, Amie Jane. *The Declaration of Independence in Translation: What It Really Means (Kids' Translations).* North Mankato, MN: Capstone Press (2018).

Learn More Online

1. Go to **www.factsurfer.com**

2. Enter "**Declaration of Independence**" into the search box.

3. Click on the cover of this book to see a list of websites.

Index

About the Author

Marcia Abramson is an editor and writer who lives in Ann Arbor, Michigan. She gets encouraging tweets—real ones—from Lemon the budgie and Phoebe the conure.